Advance Praise for *Reach Out, Reach In*

How we are made is how we see, and from the rich mosaic of her background Leah Klass delivers kaleidoscopic poems that will persuade your vision to see this world made strange and precious. This book offers local beginnings, global consciousness, and the courage to use language for what it needs to do: sustain the sovereign self engaged in connecting the private life to the public world. Enter this book troubled, then emerge knowing "there is another way." — Kim Stafford, author of *Singer Come from Afar*

I read *Reach Out, Reach In* straight through and want more. Leah Klass tells to the bone truth in bold narratives and chewable language. She is a thoroughly American woman who gathered new languages and a layered identity living in many countries. "Understand I am global," she writes, and we do, seeing through her "inherited pattern recognition" a unifying grasp of culture and language that threads through her own evolution from childhood to maturity. These brave poems move with a strong beat, riding on a wide and inclusive heart. They illuminate so much of a woman's experience through the stages of her life. For Klass, a fierce advocacy for all people developed, rooted in connection and kindness, and in her passion for acts big and small in families and communities that count toward healing the world. — Rae Latham

Reach Out, Reach In
By Leah Klass

Reach Out, Reach In
By Leah Klass

For Caitlin, who has listened to my truth desde siempre

Edited by Christopher Luna & Toni Lumbrazo Luna

Cover Art & Design by Mercer Hanau
mercerhanau.com

Published by Printed Matter Vancouver
Vancouver, Washington
printedmattervancouver.com

Copyright 2021
Leah Klass
leahklass.com

All rights reserved. No part of this publication may be reproduced, distributed, or transmitted in any form or by any means, including photocopying, recording, or other electronic or mechanical methods, without the prior written permission of the publisher, except in the case of brief quotations embodied in critical reviews and certain other noncommercial uses permitted by copyright law.

CONTENTS

I Am Made

What Are You Made Of?	9
Etymology of my Name	11
A treasure, unexpected	12
"Moonlight and music, starlight and melody"	13
Axial Points	14
Haunted Souls	16
These Thighs	17
El Corazón de La Sirena (The Heart of the Mermaid)	19

Help Yourself

My Age Defiance	23
To Avoid Danger of Suffocation	25
Playgrounds and Laughter	27
Place	28
On Interpretation	29
A Segregated Silence	30
Romance Postponed	31
Mom Rage	32
Also Known As Chad Gad Ya	34
Married for a While	36
Oh! That Quote is For Us: "Love You to the Moon and Back"	38
Jorden	39
A Different Definition	40

Healing the World

From "The News"	43
Based On Coltrane's Meditation and Resolution	44
Letter to America	47
Our New Bridge	49
In My Next Life, I'll Remember	51
Off Broadway 2007	52
Heart's Beat	54

They Are All Worth It	56
Our Name	58
Making Love What I Want	60
Take Your Hands Off! A Tribute to Planned Parenthood	62
If You Hurry	63
An Absence of Humanity	64
The Things We Dance Around	65
Christmas Dissident: December 7, 2020	67
2017 Prophecy	69
Tikkun Olam	71

Acknowledgments

About the Author

I Am Made

What Are You Made Of?

I was made of breast milk and shiny, black LPs of Elis Regina and Sergio Mendes. First in an apartment and then in a neat, brown, thousand-square-foot house with a picture window facing the street. California-style,
said my mother, as she admired the dogwood tree planted in the front yard.

I was made of crispy, hot cheese tortillas, American cheese running out from in between their brown edges and sticking to my fingers like drying Elmer's glue.

I was made during games of make-believe, hours of hiding behind bushes, rolling rocks to find pill bugs, wiping dried yellow grass stalks out of my braids and picking at the dark mud under my fingernails, as all of the girls on the block yipped and called to each other like Pilgrims, like Indians, like Astronauts, like Pirates, like Aliens, like Anne of Green Gables and Ramona Quimby. It was constant discovery on our Aleutian Islands, in our amber waves of grain, in our tropical jungles and desert sands.

I was made while I rode on the yellow banana seat of my new bicycle, Sunshine Beauty, with white double-knotted shoelaces, all the way down Westmoreland Road, whooshing by chain link fences and up and down those bumpy curbs.

I was always looking: for cars, for Sean Sweeney the Rock Thrower, for Cinnamon Jellinik cheerleading, for Leslie at home with her sister, all the way down to Westcott Road, where I didn't know the names of the neighbors anymore, just the greying paint of the house where the blind man lived next to the blue trim of the Casa de Castro.

I was made with the knowledge that Blanca and Lina's mom, dreaming of home in San Salvador, took all her sleeping pills at one time and didn't wake up again, ever. Not to the strange smells of the industrial ironing boards at the Black Tie Dry Cleaner or to her husband's clothes, stained green from so many grass clippings. I knew, too, that Brenda's dad got in trouble for writing a book about Padre Romero and couldn't go back to his country, not even if he wanted to.

I was made with the understanding that my parents worked very hard, collected aluminum from the trash on our dog walks, spent long hours on afterschool coaching jobs, all so we might have just what we had, or someday, something extra, like a trip to the beach, just imagine, the ocean, the sand or our very own box of sugary cereal.

I am still that girl, strong in character,
heart of hopefulness, filled with esperanza,
made of memories, shaped by my childhood:

I am made.

Etymology of My Name

my mother had completed her conversion   while I was in her womb
mikvah, warm water, other women, judgment   she wanted only good for me
a name that was fluid   could be used around the world   to blend in
Leee-a after Ma Lil   Laya Hebrew name, in the Bible, either way
an entry ticket to a foreign land

               blend in, fit in, find your way   she'd had more trouble

this name has served me well in Israel, the plane tires still hot from skidding to a stop on the
runway Lay-a,   all junior year, no questions asked   they say Laya, b'ivrit
and off to UVa I got to go my own way choose the vibe   I called myself then Laya
and in Brasil it rolled right off their tongues and they added more

                                       I was made Laya Maria

and on to Germany right   swift and kindly   firmly Laya!
all the while my bouncing in and out of old
of circles   places   friendships: Leeeya
my silver, gold, my Brownie rhyme of new and past time
I could tell who knew me or knew me well

Now Georgia, Denver, Portland   where to next?

Who is she: Leeee-a or Laya?

When I say it doesn't matter
what I really mean
is that I've never been sure
if I am allowed
to have it all.

A treasure, unexpected

Sometime ago, on walks to school, up Manor, Westmoreland and then Wayne
My mother pointed out that four leaves, congregated clusters, grew together, in one place.

On days of dew or rain or Mondays after Mr. Mutteman had mowed the lawn
She dared me to look down and find the small clovers, proudly sticking up to me.

Her story was that she and Uncle Eric both could find a shiny dime tossed in a field--
                                      Pattern recognition, it runs in the family.

And for the time since then I've always seen the pattern and also, that which doesn't fit;
I can't resist but stoop down, scoop up all sorts of shiny tidbits, diamond earring, crystal.

The princess cut that fell out of a wedding ring; the green glass shard that's rested dusty
for one thousand years; in the corner of an airport or in Antwerp cobblestones.

My collection now robust. Small bags of moments lost or left behind
Morsels that fill out the edges of my stories, push me toward the past.

These are your memories long lost but not forgotten. I share a secret message:
Do no fret, the emptiness, the absence, for your love no longer lives alone.

"Moonlight and music, starlight and melody"

I never knew what had gone on when Dad was away
He left early for school having shaved his head with cream from a cup
And often arrived after dark, after coaching, after dinner
And angry with things left unsaid.
We would put on the music.
It would dampen the danger.

Nothing made my father calmer
than a house filled, floating
on the a cappella rhythms
of The Persuasions.

The low shelf with its thin paper squares
held the shiny round magic of happiness.
The loud CHRK of the needle placed gently on the edge
the soft click of the button and that magical metal arm
that took us into the music.

My mom welcomed us with arms open wide.
Jorge Ben Jor cantava em palavras que eu nem entendia
Ay Ay Carambaaaaaa, Galileu na Galileia
These were her records, recordings of another época, another lugar.
Remembrances of her other self and a time in Brazil that I would seek and live later on.

If the silver Technics was my family's greatest investment
It was only because the vibrations that echoed from the speakers
Acted as a balm to soothe us, fumigated against angst, anger and worry
They brought Caetano together with Marvin Gaye and Joni Mitchell and The Spinners
They brought all of us together to dance toward hope.

Como dizia isso é o que é amor. "Like they say, that's what love is." (Jorge Ben)

Axial Points

                                        Desperately I crammed
                                        my hands into the plastic
                                        cavities of an airplane bathroom
                                        as wide as
                                        in between my shoulders.

I had bled through my shorts.

                                        Remarkable, not quite sixteen,
                                        all on my own, middle seat, squeeze
                                        past one man,
                                        two, body odor, fried potatoes,
                                        dressed in black with greasy hair,
                                        grunts unfriendly, dour, really.

My blood was on the seat cushion.

                                        Sweaty palms and pasty hair and teenage angst
                                        and foreign countries, all alone, I sat with
                                        scratchy airline paper towels between my legs
                                        for seven hours.

I had not prepared for this.

                                        Arrival, *sdrawkcab* letters, no vowels, harsh sounds,
                                        soldiers, side arms, salty air, strange names,
                                        distractions!

I had bled and lost my luggage.

                                        Meeting hosts, the principal, a chaperone,
                                        other kids, on the bus and off the bus, hot showers,
                                        gifted maxi pads and clothing and that night,
                                        a welcome celebration.

I would bleed, I would survive.

At the introduction, roses, names called, other teens,
some beaming, joined new cliques, relaxed, my turn,
stand up, walk forward, HEY, OUCH, he tripped me!

With strength of lions up I shot, reared back, all teeth
and kicked Yaron, so smug, right squarely, in his stomach.

Surprise!

The crowd erupted, cheering, came to hug me,
praise me, wished they'd done that – shown that bully.

I had taken charge,
protecting self,
that kind of power,
always heroic,
full moon courage.

Haunted Souls

Beware
my mom said
I know it sounds like
I'm taking their side
but I want you to listen
before you use
your voice.

If you are too angry

        and I know, for a woman, that's angry at all

If you are too straight forward

        and I know, I was taught to save the truth for later

If you are too much your own person

        and I wonder, the self I am just learning to be?

I think you are wonderful
said my mom

just beware.

These Thighs   for Diane di Prima

When I was younger my mother
prepared us for the swimming pool.
Her warm hand, it cupped, reassuringly,
all the way from shoulder
down my arm to the elbow
her eyes honest as she said,

"These thighs:
there are only two types of thighs
those that always touch
and those that never will.
Be proud of your legs,
they are strong."

And a teenage me with a soft belly,
hurting for its lack of self-confidence,
would try to ignore
those thighs above those knees
and those feet on the floor.

The boys, all they noticed – those jugs
a nickname, a testosterone game.
It was these thighs
that walked me away
to my confident place – to save face.

These thighs:
At the University, Charlottesville,
on the Lawn, no pants on
Thomas Jefferson, legacies,
run like the spring night breeze!
These toned, shaved, and daring thighs carried me, streaking,
past thrilled frat boy eyes.

It was a win, no pressure,
not so much, to be thin,

with thighs that don't touch.

These thighs:
On a boat deck, serene,
off the coast of São Paulo,
Brazilians, their thighs – realized,
lives of luxury, waxed and tanned
all the way up to round beauties
of butt cheeks both polished
and perfect – lording over legs
and proclaiming, "she IS a queen!"

I rolled up the corners of my modesty,
hoping my thighs might say the same.

These thighs:
Closest confidantes of that
mythical cave of creation.
The gifting of body from mother to child remains something savage
a total submission to the needs
of this instant.

These thighs:
Oh, they've walked the world
and whispered to each other
through pains now forgotten.
How fortunate in their fondness.

Now I, like my mother,
share the wisdom –
none other than
the knowledge
of two types of thighs.

El Corazón de La Sirena: The Heart of the Mermaid

Diga-me
what is the moment
en cual momento
that you decide to
switch, flick, click
or is it to open?   abrir
to hear the voices   a dentro
a thought   pensamiento?

What in your cerebro
collides with emociones
your heartbeat un grito
the ticitac of tacones.

How many cultural identities can you please?

Hermana, mi Argentina
Brasileira, Yanqui, Norteña
café con leche, mira pa' bajo (look down!)
de la Frontera, that's a wall to you…
Espere! Fences keep locos out of el Zoo
do you know which side you are on, which is you?
I walk by growling, hands hidden, nodding Sí,
Animales del Norte, keep them lejos de mi.

Por favor, understand who I am is global
all the languages, tickets to life, Carnaval,
mi aparencia, it was not my choice,
what I got: education, amor and a voice.

Paso por paso, tides of words and ideas,
map out understandings, explain away fears
fabulous fables, murals of belief
viajes guided by calls from the deep.
La larga avenida in my heart
always lead me to mi.

Help Yourself

My Age Defiance

"You probably have a snack somewhere in your purse," he said.

                                                               "Because you're a mom."

But what I pulled out were kind words and a smile – traded that
     for my dismay and a thunderclap across his face.

In the bottom of my purse I have a plastic bag: a Ziploc of desires.
It's filled with Peter Jordan, only the first half of our Argentine romance.
I tore the paper where he started to spin webs of doubt and kept the sheepskin rugs
and the violin and some red wine, malbec.

I've also got the paystub from the last big job I did not take. Barcelona keys to apartments
where I'd left my black mesh stockings drying on the line.
The late morning sun shining; bougainvillea covered whitewashed walls;
fresh orange juice pressed and poured into a glass; a slice of baguette waiting for me
to add butter. Coffee so strong it knocked me off my ass.

Way down in the corner, my crumpled smudged belief in peace and freedom, from
wiping bottoms and tying laces and remembering and reminding and recording it all.

A time I used to know, I'd ride my bike, with shiny fenders and a honking horn,
right through Cheesman Park. Watch gay men flirt in the shadows of white columns,
Park Police hand tickets to the owners of dogs who'd dropped the leash. I'd park in front of
the World Trade Center and snake the lock through chrome spokes before zooming up
twenty-seven floors to work.

Here too, a sharps container, small and round, for instruments I've used to cause pain
in sisters – make them question who they are and yes, love me, too. I may have hurt my
chances for winning that prize; I didn't post the letter; I didn't board the bus; I didn't
practice hard enough or turn in my words on time. And here's a painful heartache that I
never felt.

A crinkled bag of love now. That is where I've gone to get your answer
about those snacks. Used up all my magic to turn those memories
of who I was before I birthed those babies

into an open bag of peanut flavored crunch,
and melty salty goodness,
it's all right here.

I'm a mom now. I carry a purse.
Are you hungry for a life well-lived?   Help yourself.

To Avoid Danger of Suffocation

They say that you should never give a baby a plastic bag.
The warning, in bold black letters is printed on the side of the very bag
you would never consider putting over anyone's head, especially not a baby's
but maybe
your own?

That is how I have felt on and off,
for the last 5 years of my life.
As if I have been living under a plastic bag.

My oxygen is limited. My thoughts are slimy and stagnant
like condensation, trapped. In fact,
all of my new and bright ideas have gone
up! from my brain down! onto my tongue out! of my lips,
sometimes moist, sometimes dry and then
they're gone.

Out and up, out and away from my body ready to interact with the world when:
FLUP!
they hit the plastic,
fail to evaporate, to penetrate, to germinate.
They just cling, become cloudy and lukewarm.
They inch toward each other,
as they creep they lose their original form, their identity, their…

Occasionally I will be lost in thought,
and will be   surprised!
SHAKE OPEN WIDE EYES
when a droplet of something
like a bead of sweat
from someone
else's race
trails a memory
across my face
it's a salty
stale

taste
on my
tongue

the flavor of something
that used to be.

Playgrounds and Laughter

Hello, my name is
He's so cute how old is
Oh you too and mine is
If you have ideas I will, yes
Let's make a plan, here is my
We all want to,
well…

Maybe that last line's a lie
Can't speak for those fools
and they'll find an excuse
for not once ever
asking your name
as you stand at the side
of the stairs to the playground
your hair in a cotton cloth wrap
and your white teeth shone
in a magnetic smile
eyes glossy from blinking in the sun
and your child so darling and friendly
like a hug two feet tall, with caffeine
No, they don't mean
to ignore you
my love.

They just don't know
how to care.

Place

In my bed at night
legs in front
feet keeping each other company
under soft cotton sheets.
Kids coughing in the other room
husband snoring, totally out.
In my head, a ball of twine
wound up worries and a kitten of creativity.

I want to lose myself in the lists
I want to go online
I want to scroll down until my eyes hurt
until my vision blurs
I want to hear the incessant whirr of the cars moving on down on the highway
I want to know that my money earned, set, saved will buy me
a vacation
a creamy new lipstick
a pair of leather boots for the next new season.
I do not want to worry
about turning off the lamp by my bed
so that the pickers going through my bin
won't see my face in the window
as I watch them sift through envelopes, offers, opportunities
and go on their way to sell my
name
address
identity.

Maybe the new me
her raspy voice at the end of the line
all shiny credit cards
and no worries
will buy that vacation
to Mexico?

On Interpretation

My little daughter danced to a song.
Enrique Iglesias reaching deep down into
a reservoir of cultural chaos
heated waters of love and longing.

The dance makes her happy
glee is the size of her smile
and Sheila, from Portland,
her loving, adopted, neighborhood grandma
remarks that *all* songs in Spanish
have the word CORAZÓN in them.

I'd object, but my tongue, twisted citrus
and my chest, lleno, pesado,
have already dissolved,
they followed an outline of me,
In a dive
down a soul list of language
to my own CORAZÓN.

This is not page turning
square corners
or a whitened smile,
polite distance between tu y yo
this is years of garnacha and coffee
this is tips of fingers once calloused from so much violin practice
then savory from the line in the factory, Zeitia
where the Hebrew word Zayit
means olive and in Castellano, oil, aceite is made of aceitunas
and the words lap around the edges of the Mediterranean
casting a spell on all of the children who play in their waters.

Yes, all songs have the word CORAZÓN in them.
So do the daughters who dance.

A Segregated Silence

Looking out onto the gray expanse
of the cul-de-sac
solitary and silent under the heat of the August sun.

This is the isolation of suburbia
that you dreamed about
no corner hydrant fiestas
no yellowed curtains pushed aside by Buela's
wrinkled hands,
high in a window shouting down
to little nietos.

No hot oil smell or questions about crema
or revuelta, no grease-coated fingers or
rolled up balls of aluminum.

The back of your air-conditioned forearm
has forgotten how to wipe off
summer's sweat.

Your neighbors hide inside,
you've never been in there.

They spend their PhDs, their CFOs,
on upgrades and their renovations,
all are done by brown and dark-skinned bodies
wielding loud machines and hopeful smiles
tinny salsa played on prepaid cell phones
and when they've gone
you look around and turn
inside yourself.

This segregated silence, a blessing or a curse?

Romance Postponed

My husband's fiftieth birthday
is coming up in January.

I've been saving some money
and dreaming of one week away
from the kids.

We've never done that.

We've had one night
at the coast in a rainstorm,
had to drive in that weather,
and together believed
we would die
at Hug Point.

We spent two nights
in Córdoba, Spain.
Touring in 112 degree heat
and at night bitten on the ass
by fire ants.

My mother told me on Friday
that she honestly does not want
to watch our girls.

I could lament the lack of a doting grandma.
But a whole week away?

Just imagine what could go wrong!

Mom Rage

At the table   they sit waiting   take out boxes open   releasing steam

scent of basil   hot pepper's twang   and they've sat down   at their places

and they're waiting   for my sign. My head turns right   and around the corner

I see my mistake   a habit 'mal'   and I observe   the covered counters

feel my insides   filling up   as if the faucet   of my anger   overfloweth my
        inner sink

each cup is shouting   each fleck of noodle   each tiny pile   of flour sugar

each smear   each dollop dried   and stuck and staring   they mock me teasing

they tell me   look here   No matter how long   you try   to escape us   you are unable
        we will call you out

about your sadness   out about your angst   out about how solitary   this confinement

and its mundane emphasis   has left you empty   has made you fearful

of the thing you love the most.   We will tie you   to this job   that you don't want

to this house   that would be calm   to this moment   that would be wonderful.   If you
        only cleaned   and shined

and washed   and filled   and emptied   and placed   and dried   and set

and all the anger   rose up inside me   lit like gas   a bomb of flames

I am no mother   I am an animal   I am not loving   my words destroy from mouth to air   from air to table   rage covers loved ones   and it extinguishes

all of their joy. The food is cold now   the kids are crying   so I go   to wash the dishes

numb to all   that makes me sad.

Also Known As Chad Gad Ya

At this year's Passover Seder
a wispy wild woman named Donna
invited us all to sit quietly
and think about something
we'd held on to all year long.

Some burr in our paws
that spare shard of glass we'd held
under our tongue.

On this night, could we relax
and set it on the table?

Or catch it and turn it over tenderly
to see what it said?

Through each prayer, she suggested
we could walk away from that weight
and this Seder, like all
was first a labored plodding
then a skip and soon
a quick run
a long night as it were.

My wish met resistance
to cease with my worry
the constant tensing of social muscles
impeding my fun.

And so I drank the wine – AMEN!
I let the kids make noise – AMEN!
I ate too much soup – AMEN!
I drank more wine again – AMEN!

With each prayer
I emptied my apron pockets

of so many stones
and sank more deeply
into my chair.

Finally, we all sang Chad Gad Ya
and I laughed until I cried
as Naomi bleated
like a goat.

Four and a half hours later
I rose to go home,
buoyed by joy
and free to love myself.

Married for a While

My husband is
early afternoon time
voluptuous.

He is rounded warm belly
pleasure
a nod to Botero.

He's worked for years just to achieve
the perfect soft fuzz cap of curly hair
evenly, thickly, absolutely
all over
his body.

He leaves me a love note in curly Q,
on each white surface of the house.

At night, when I miss him, I reach for the
transparent tube and I trace figure eights
from the CPAP machine to the face mask and Flip!
up the cotton-lined cup
that is hiding his lips
and their sharp peppered
dusting of beard.

He breathes me in and
we sink like two sandbags
our skin hot from the sun--
we sink into the mattress and
twist like a licorice,
braiding and melting
our bodies
together.

We've been married for a while.

Ours is a pleasure
far greater than
your first glance
or
even your second
might reveal.

Oh! That Quote is For Us
"Love You to The Moon and Back" for Holly

Hey Girl,
Meet me at the corner of this:

Where the Church and the frisbee golf course collide.
Where the ivy invaders still climb power lines.

Meet me between doing for the kids and
doing for the clients and
we'll share a balm of neighborhood gossip.

Laugh about the Donald Trump your dog left in your slippers,
Laugh about my neighbor's domestication of raccoons
and my newfound love for taxidermy.

We will laugh and we will remember
floating up above --
how friendship launches love
up to the moon.

Jorden

I saw her in the basement hallway
at the gym.
Her red-rimmed eyes puffy against
her milky skin.
Never had I noticed her freckles.
"Would you like a hug?" I asked,

Closer now, I stepped as she sat
at the end of the couch.

Before, she had only stood
behind the counter, welcoming
ushering, organizing things.

"Oh – I'm fine," she replied.
"But I'll take a hug anyway."

And she pushed up off the armrest
and our bodies came together
like a pillow and your head.
We relaxed and stood softly
for a moment of humanity
almost strangers
and I thought about my sisters
far away.

A Different Definition

Talking to my neighbors is hard:
their daughters glance shyly
at me mowing my lawn
under the boughs
of the giant sequoia.

They cross the street
when I walk my dog
wearing shorts and
exposing my legs
unshaven.

Their limbs are covered
with thick fabric
even in summer months.

Those girls are the same age as mine
and I secretly wish I could spirit them away
to teach them
about climate change
and birth control
and tolerance
and modern dance
democracy
and poetry
written by women
like me
who are searching
for the words
to express
our belief
that there is
always
another way.

Healing the Whole World

From "The News"

The last white rhino died this week
after years of sweet hay, special pats,
encouragement from biologists

desperate attempts to help him
ejaculate into a receptacle

       anything

to keep the species alive

The last white rhino was shot to death

He'd gone outside his enclosure

       to smoke a cigarette
       on his back porch

Those cops won't go to court
but they're suspended now

A few paid days of leave, vacating
watching reruns of *Roseanne* on TV

In textbooks, Nature is defined as

       something unsafe —
       caged for its own sake

like every good dead thing
we'll soon forget

       You were taught to do that too

Based on Coltrane's "Meditation" and "Resolution"

Looking over this watery grave
this midnight jazz
I've been there – in this club
but I will never belong – this culture is not my song.

This is not my culture, this is not my culture
to recite the hellish happening of my fathers and
my forefathers – my mothers who have had to
substitute for them for so long and on and on
throughout the chill of dark street corners
and constant mourning.

My culture is taught to fear
and to read, to use study to impede
to stem the bleeding from collective heads
shaved down.

We are taught to blend, to assess, to patch our needs together,
quickly mending before the anxiety has a space to creep in.

Sadness, this is my culture:
forgiveness, atonement,
lest we, lest we
lest we forget.

I am trained to suck in my breath s-l-ow-l-y
to walk with my knowledge of the past
tucked under my arm tightly
to check for exits, to count the rows
to call for help and to trust myself.

I know my mother cared about me.
She cared so much it hurts me and
and the warm embrace, part passion
part passionate guilt
the sweet and salty tears

genetic passing down, healing heat,
like steam from the soup pot.

This muse, these historic names, these Friday night lights, this talk of tribe
a recognition, this gift of being an outsider, cherished, understood, explained:
my culture.
That other, that loss, that constant question mark of mothers
those ships that sailed down into darkness
those millions stretched out thin over blue spheres, wet and deserted.

Where the music evaporated
where in working over the Earth
        they forgot their own names
where Spanish moss bore silent witness
where the mother tongue was lashed
where the whip cut grooves
and the mines were states away.

Whale bone beams
in the Catholic churches
silver crosses spirited by priests
all the crimson velvet of their robes
colored by your blood.

Boys stretched into men on journeys forced
men turned into boys by patriarchal demons
unfailing in their judgment, hardened in their hatred.

So kneaded, so beaten, so rolled,
so rounded, so softened, so saddened,
now unrecognizable in their form
covered in the coating of their hellish happenings
inside ever empty
the archetypal loss of mothers
imagining their return
like the hills above the Neahkanie mountain

might imagine the return of prehistoric sequoias
as their soil crumbles, cascades, landslides
into the Pacific Ocean.

Looking over this watery grace
this midnight jazz
I've been here, in this club
but I will never belong
this culture is not my song.

Letter to America

I am everything because of you. My friends tell me they don't care,
no loyalty for them. They'll move elsewhere before the hammer falls.

Me: I'm a bit overcooked for that. I see death in each worn and gray patch of sidewalk.
I yank on the dog's leash in front of the neighbor's overgrown yard.

Why do I care if my middle is soft and doughy and peeks out above my jeans?
How much time do I spend organizing my closet? Mostly rows of clothes from the second
hand store, as if excess is excused when using cast-offs. That's consumerism.

That's addiction.
That is mine.

Ryan almost died from cancer three years ago.

His mom called and we zoomed downtown filling garbage bags with expired cereal and
appliances NIB--that's New In Box. Paper boxes of plastic bags and plastic bottles of
vitamins. And he didn't die then.

He survived the chemo, rekindled a romance, had a baby, lived in Brooklyn. And it took me
3 trips and 5 calls and aching hours to get the management company to forgive the dying
man's one parking ticket. Our van, his last black night in Portland. Death placed the green
notice snug against our windshield. Death paved the roads with asphalt. Death was in the
homeless eyes staring blankly at my car window. Union Station underpass.

We move them, those stains on our green communal lawns. We move them like we move
the ants in our kitchen, the killdeer nests at our school. We mow their tents down quickly,
with a loud noise and the smell of diesel, reminder to all: Black Gold, that's the real God.
All powered—Cars are powered, grills are powered, weed wackers and earth movers and
chain saws, why, they are powered and power.

The chemicals, the closets, the cancer, these causes, this country.
I am so American that I have confused the progression.

Use them, destroy them, burn them, trash them, dump them, exterminate them, yes,
fix it all up   by cutting it down.

Don't be afraid
of progress.

It's all you've ever known.

Our New Bridge

Holding out a dented cup
aside his cardboard sign
at the crux of the
Ross Island Bridge on-ramp
in rush hour slowdown
stands someone's soul.

No longer laughing
this soul is now naked
and void of color
empty for all to ignore.

If that patch of gravel
if that grey curb were filled up
that soul covered with all its past:
love and hugs and bubbling
glasses of root beer and icy cold popsicles
summer-stained overalls
and boards hammered high
around an oak tree trunk!

Oh! If that soul had pink
birthday candles and new
cotton socks and minty fresh
breath and straight as the day
the braces came off teeth
and as sure as before Vietnam
and as clever as without
caffeine or a smoke
a peach-fuzzy softness
and a raspberry smile.

If that soul were covered
in sunshine
in all that you love
would you stop

and make eye contact?

In My Next Life, I'll Remember

You might win a Pulitzer Prize for misprizing
the unencumbered garbs of Philistine guests.

Their languished marches
granules of blistering history
seared into the crevices
of the pedestrian mind.

You might gain sackfuls of troubled opportunity
disguised as velvety desires,
laden with pyritic philosophies
sparkling in the deserts of thought
the tumbling beckoning
heat waves of an oasis.

You might reach colorful cliffs of knowledge
as the floodwaters of mediocrity rise
acting out the rubbery flesh of No. 2 pencils on the page –
with a grade schooler's eagerness to please a tired tyrant
wreaking havoc on the stick figure that you almost were.

Now a memory   quickly fading
as the beasts burst forth
from cinderblock enclosures
loud bells clanging
earthen clodding
sheer elation rising.

You might (hiccup) die
dusty as you settle
into plastic permanence
a recycled soul.

Off Broadway, 2007

In Baker, my hood, Denvertown
too young to know the role I played
my 30-year-old ignorance
thick like fat
in liquid form
next door, moans, guttural
and a squeak as a
creampuff of a person
not 3 years large
toddles into the yard
like the last piece of cake
on the plate.

Through the screen door, I watch.
She climbs up two steps onto my porch
Her line-drawing chalk hands
dusty, careless
open-mouthed syllables
soaked in saliva
big plump lips
salty boogers drying
pants stained and full
with no one there to notice
not even me.

Creaking screen doors
banging on their frames
cops cruising in shiny cars
that left hand searchlight
eyeballing it all
those weeds rising up
through river rock gardens
a chipped and peeling
white-washed ramp
a wheelchair's view
this crooked house

this mangy cat
these neglected neighbors
two blocks from Broadway

I had no idea
what my shallow roots
would displace.

Heart's Beat

"Did you know that I was on a diet?" asked John.
No, I thought.
I am self-medicating with dark chocolate.

I met un pibe at a party once who claimed to be a vampire.
We were in Buenos Aires, in someone's tiny apartment,
smoke thicker than air and I laughed out loud
when I saw he'd filed his teeth into points.
Then I went outside to call a cab. Venga!

There was a pizza place on the corner outside of the Jardín Botánico
where the policia came in one night, but we all had our papers,
only Juan was scared--he'd seen this before--
        and decided to leave for Spain.

One plane ticket was a year's salary
and he had to buy a round trip
so that they'd believe
he was going to come home.

Did you know that there's a truck stop
on the edge of the Black Foot Reservation
where all the local ladies go for sewing supplies?

The porcupine quills are mostly from round there
picked up from roadside accidents.

The eye candy are tubes full of glass beads and tanned hides
for moccasin making and all the bear claws and hawk talons
that you never knew to dream of.

Maybe it doesn't cross your mind
when your feet cross the street—the thought I mean,
that you could say "hello" and "how are you?"

In a different way, a way with no stop signs or tender fears,
an open way, a fluid way, the way that leads to friendship,
or something like respect.

They Are All Worth It

Juan Antonio has too few teeth, too much bad luck and accidently spread the weed killer at the home that is rented out to no one. His teeth hurt and he still smiles. OHSU has a low-cost dental clinic. Here's the number. Juan who always waves. Every Tuesday when he comes to cut the grass, until the big mistake, the lawn is poisoned, and then he is gone.

Maribel is a custodian at my daughter's elementary school. She is bursting with good energy. She has a two-year-old daughter who goes to daycare far away in Hillsboro, which is complicated for her mom. Maribel always speaks to me in Spanish even though we both speak English perfectly well. She hugs me, careful not to touch my clothes with the plastic gloves she wears on her hands, for she is in the cafeteria, helping small children separate their compost from their trash.

Flor M. is a mom at my kids' school. She is a mom who heard me speaking in Spanish in 2017 and asked if it was true. Was it true that ICE was rounding up immigrants at the transit center? She wanted to go to Fred Meyer and buy food for her kids, they were hungry. Now she is afraid. She moved away. Facebook tells me that she is still around, somewhere.

Vicky and I met rolling down a hill laughing after having crashed a party in college. I planned her honeymoon in Chile when I lived there. She got a medical degree while her husband was traveling for work. She divorced him when he was home. Now her schedule is full, her patients demanding. She has little time for the unfinished search, the research for herself.

Eliza is a friend who always looks strong, stands up straight, has her hair brushed and smiles. She is even-tempered and kind and should be in charge. Eliza is married to Max, who rode a bull bareback when his first daughter was born. He was more scared of the baby. He's now taught her to ski and to climb and I'm sure that baby is Eliza's daughter, for she doesn't fear anything at all.

Mara, a teacher, has a head of grey curls with shining strands of black. She sews thoughtful bright colors through snippets of textiles. Her healings are woven into quilts, which warm kindred souls, who too suffer broken hearts.

Caitlin lives at the foot of grand mountains. Majestic in her posture, her smile a daybreak, her red hair a sunset. She has conquered foreign lands by learning their sizzle and pop. Her compassion and culinary skills invite the flavors of the world into her house and her kindness makes it impossible to leave.

These people are mine. They are all worth it.

Our Name

While she was in kindergarten
at the end of the school year

when the peonies were
starting to droop over

bowing into heavy
fragrant poses

her Dadu walked her out
of the cul-de-sac

and down the hill
to the open space

where friends meet
in the morning.

She was so full of thankful
so full like the cup of milk

she'd practiced pouring and
her mother sometimes yelled about

when she got distracted
and it almost went over the edges.

She hugged her father's jeans
and looked back to her friends

bouncing down the tile hallway
as he left for his bus.

She knew happy was a way
to describe her feelings.

She knew that pride meant
country and father.

She did not understand why anyone
would dislike her dad or call him names.

She thought he was the best doctor ever
though mother did not explain
the meaning of EEO complaints
or discriminatory hiring practices

but she knew that it was like
being pushed out of her chair by the other kids

when they heard her teacher
try to say her name.

Making Love What I Want

It starts off like that
the leather shoe on your socked foot
a misstep on the wet path
a fall-en-leaf

you slip and on the way down
feel the heat rise up, embarrassment
and whoosh

you're on your back, your khaki pants
are starting to soak through
you laugh.

It starts off like a grandmum
who is standing up the path
on a Sunday afternoon
wiping her hands upon her apron
reaching back into the house
for a big, fluffy towel
the kind with pink and orange diamonds
that is usually by the pool
she's looked outside whilst baking
and heard from the clouds
that you might come home wet.

It starts off like the cold metal wire
of the farm fencing
and the calf splooshes across the pen gingerly
big black marble eyes, steam huffing from her wet nose
and she knows you've brought a handful of alfalfa
and she likes you so you watch in wonder
as her fat purple tongue
stretches further than it needs to go
feel the warm slobber   feel nature's kiss.

Wouldn't it be nice if it started off
like a safe hug of memory
enveloping every tastebud of your body
in a kind and calm embrace?

Take Your Hands Off!
A Tribute to Planned Parenthood

Take your hands off me might not be a phrase familiar to **everyone**
A woman would know it for sure, and a girl maybe. Everyone **deserves**
Kind and respectful treatment, but all things are not **equal**
Even the wealthy and well-to-do limit their daughter's **access**
Young women sitting shyly, short painted nails tapping **to**
Other young people through a screen, easier in emojis than **sexual**
Understanding, more comfortable with asking Google **and**
Reading Twitter than talking with an adult about **reproductive**
Health. He's just a friend from the internet, she'd said, not linking **health**
And his touch. No one had ever spoken about care, **reproductive**
Nor about her body being her own, they only offered reactions, **services**
Directions to clinics and bus rides and lying to parents **and**
Suddenly she saw it, friendly faces and hugs and explanations, **education**
Older women willing to talk about boys and breasts and self-**care**
Funny thing, how they had taught her to say **no**
Funny that after all she'd been through, she heard them say, "You **matter**."
!&$@ed up, I say. How come nobody else had cared for her, no matter **what**.

Everyone deserves equal access to sexual and reproductive health care services and education. Planned Parenthood's slogan is "Care. No matter what."

If You Hurry

In Spanish, the word refúgio means shelter, safety.
It is something parents seek for their children in a storm,
It is something the persecuted seek during war.
When you drop the re- it means fugitive.

How quickly those seeking shelter
were turned into evil.

Refúgio: Shelter.
Fúgio: Fugitive.

This is all turned around.

If you hurry across borders, across cultures, across deserts and rivers
you may be able to find something, something better.
If you hurry   Vaya con Dios.

Tarde: Late.
Arde: Burns.

The mass of bodies leaning North, leaning into rejection.
Just a policy: "go now" work quietly, hide away until the next administration.
The tides are changing, they have to.

Sola: Alone.
Ola: Wave.

We all want this.
We all want the same thing.
Why do you act so surprised?
Our biggest blind spot is our memory:
our inability to connect our past
to our future.

Vida: Life.
Ida: Going/One Way/Departure.

An Absence of Humanity

as a child I would visit my grandparents every week / they would teach me 'bout their childhood / saying nothing 'bout how easy my life was compared to theirs / they would show me black and white photos of a time we dressed in rags / in the ghetto that meant we could not live anywhere we liked / in the ghetto that meant we could not hold any job we pleased / jews in europe in the ghetto / that's why savta saved her money to send to cousins in palestine / in the days when eggs were rationed the cousins saved coupons for a year to make a cake for yona's wedding / out of the ghetto and into cold blue waters crossing british soldiers patrolling desert marauders raiding / time for a kibbutz / my saba taught me hebrew on the weekends never talking 'bout no gods other than microscopes / my savta taught me speaking out against oppression was the rule / that women had to change the ways of men who came before them / that children could learn anything and anything they learned was like a magic power / couldn't take it from them / so the learning and the hebrew and the history and the protest all went hand in hand in hand / the color of the law and all the laws of the religion used to rule the people / those came later / the persecution and the killing and the concentration camps / those came later / the days my elementary friends went off to college and came back deciding labels should define us / those came later / the realization that the little things / the courtesies / the hugs / the meals / the nods / adult approval and accepting and belonging / those the things / the decencies whose absence will betray democracy / the everyday in house and hood / in school / on street / in shop / the ghetto doesn't happen overnight / the camps and the killing doesn't happen overnight / it's micro / our aggressions and the sense that we can't change them / it's macro / forgetting 'bout how easy our lives are compared to theirs

The Things We Dance Around
After Suzanne La Grande

Remember the night you didn't have to wait
to lean on the wall and watch the others dance
that Friday late in dark D.C.
IDs checked at the door
glowing from your preparations
perfumed and nervous
about cumbia y salsa, Colombiana o Boriqua
unwilling to wait on the wall again
ready pá bailar con los boys
finally feeling free, feeling sexy
until that visit to the bathroom
your confidence disappeared, as had your panty liner

What to do? Stand back against the wall? NO!
dance all around the white pad on the floor
the only one who refused to see it.

The Things We Dance Around

I don't have anything with which to hurt you
I only have questions

My brother André tells me that I might not even
understand you because we do not share values
and perhaps that is okay

I do things because I want to spread real love
and you talk trash, provoke and bully
I used to be caught up in that
but now I know there is no hiding
not with money or with guns, neither will work
and you profit, live off both

I can only hurt you with my love
because while I am busy working, sowing, gifting
your hate will be smothered by my success

Christmas Dissident
December 7, 2020

> *Too-qua-stee, born in the Cherokee Nation in Georgia in 1829, was a poet,*
> *lawyer and a scholar of languages*

The Bombing of Pearl Harbor
was today. All those years ago.
Not that long ago.

Dear Too-qua-stee:
That I write you, tapping tips
on plastic parts that lift and dip
made of material from deep in the Earth
does all this suction impact her girth?

I write not with feather or quill
Such extravagant animal sacrifice
Feels too close to home, I like detached, you know?
I can ignore oil stains on snow.
This is not lost on me
humanly irony.

> Detective Necessary,
> Where is the missing dignity?
> Why this we should check…
>
> I don't believe it was secured on deck
> It may have gone down
> with the wreck.

True dignity is like an evergreen tree
Standing proudly and whispering softly from afar
Silent as chopped, serene when riding on a train car
All around us this evergreen still stands (as we erect him anew)
On freshly, hastily, greedily denuded lands.

His dignity it may wane once nailed and glued, secured inside
These buildings that we live in, "Hush!" Inside their walls is a memory
Of dignity, inside this home you built with pride
As your pride plastered over what had been a tree
As you cut it down thinking of you and not he
As you dragged it along the forest, snowy path
As you [not] thought, the snowy path would last.

This year the fires came, no ball from the sky
But sparked by a lack of feeling, dignity run dry
Evergreen's smoke choked us, settled down from above
Our toxic actions contrast with an easy breathing love.

> Detective Author, prolific letter writer
> I hear your grievances, truth and pain
> Damage long past done, stolen lands of cult and gain.

Twinkling stars in a sky far away
Three million light years and 79 dark years today
We continue to sink like our ship made of morals
The heat of our hatred bleaches more brains than corals.

And our dignity, our natural wisdom, shrunk in plain sight
It now hangs like an ornament on Christmas night.
Small plastic memories
Brief yearly visitors
Empty shells of values
Linking us,
linking me and you
Too-qua-stee
to a once native land.

2017 Prophecy

I am asking the people who listen to the words I speak to forget:
Forget what they know and forego these conclusions,
these commercials, these illusions.

This propaganda telling us "turn right." This voice incessant, telling us
from somewhere in a hard metal corner with a flashing black vinyl tape
on an outdated machine it is telling us that the word is our skin; that the word is our heart;
that the word that they choose
is the one we must use and
                                     this poetry is a vision:

a comet hanging in the sky, tail in the other universe:
this garage door is slowly closing on our ability to exit, code forgotten.

You aren't locked out! You are locked in!
Precious moments these time-flying-ear-pounding-anger-filled days.

I went down to the library to check out some new perspective and
even the feminists were falling over cardboard boxes of strap-ons,
like this AR-15 fantasy was something to desire.
This voice is vocab is violence and sex and death of these I am sure.

> The Aldermen sit at their tables drinking dirt from Styrofoam cups so white that they hold all the power. Black gold – now that's power consumed. Coffee and oil and ebony and everything finite. The fortune teller reads the residual sacred grounds as the First Nation peoples freeze to death in their watery teepees and soldiers watch porn on their cellphones in tanks.

Fuck me. Poetry hasn't changed me at all this semester. I have changed poetry.
Fallen victim to the same angst that plagues our politics, swallowed the spiked
and jagged glass shards of a nation on fire.

This too is a cycle.   These ashes will clear.
In Bali, the volcano is seen as an omen. Our fields will emerge fertile.
The absence of echoes has thrown off the eagle
and her flight on the thermals has yet to take place.

Love yourself.
Love somebody.

Look up at the light and
prepare to insist that
you're not giving up.

Tikkun Olam

Healing the world
the whole world
her round, warm belly
her soft hills and her jagged cliffs
her deep pools and her hot center

Healing and nourishing her babies
responding to their cries
such endless work
for those mamalehs
this bearing witness

Softening
so that the men might too
more than freeze or melt
might soften themselves
find peace

Healing the wounded
and the suffering
lending a hand
an open palm

Joining in a moment of wonder
gifting a wash of hope
breathing in green, lush, moist
breathing out kindness, love

Healing the world
not only my world
not only our world

Healing the whole world
the WHOLE world
the world as one
Tikkun Olam.

Acknowledgments

The creativity expressed in these pages is due to the life experiences I have shared with many amazing people. I would like to thank every sweet supporter who offered me encouragement as the Covid-19 pandemic took hold. Through phone calls and Zoom meetings your assistance was warm and kind.

I would like to thank the friends who talked and listened, who questioned and laughed for countless hours of revisions and arrangements over the phone and computer, as if we were in fifth grade again working to piece together a giant collage on a posterboard sign, passing notes to each other and giggling most of the way.

My modern relationship with poetry stems from a weekly, accessible and supportive group of people who were brought and held together by Christopher Luna at the Multnomah Arts Center in Portland, Oregon. He has taught me to be grateful. It is in the act of great teaching that the teacher imparts courage. It is in the act of true learning that the student becomes brave.

I would like to hug all of the best friends I have made in the bright classroom at the bottom of the ramp in Multnomah Arts Center. You evolved from neighbor-colleagues to friends and confidantes, sharing bagels and homemade treats and fresh fruit and joy in our hours writing and sharing poetry.

I would like to thank the community artists and the non-profit workers, all the bright spirits who taught me that there is nothing more worthy than being true to yourself, no matter what. You have taught me that doing what you love is always worthwhile. I love you all. My work is a direct product of our friendships.

Speaking of truth, endless gratitude goes to my husband and daughters, and to my parents, as we work to debate and discuss and act together to make the world a more welcoming place, a world of more effective communication and peace, in which awareness leads to positive change. I love you.

About the Author

Born in Washington, D.C., Leah's education has included attending diverse public schools and studying abroad. She learned Spanish in the homes of her friends in Falls Church, Virginia. In high school she turned 16 on a secular kibbutz, where she worked on the assembly line in an olive factory and was chased by ostriches. She later waitressed and cleaned houses to help pay for her studies in Anthropology at the University of Virginia which included a year of study abroad in Brazil. She completed a master's degree in International Peace and Conflict Resolution at the University of Queensland thanks to a Rotary Fellowship in Argentina and Australia.

She spent the first years of her career bringing businesses from different countries together and encouraging friendships between strangers. Market research and report writing were a ticket to long weekends in Chile and high speed taxi rides in Mexico. She has also helped get social services to migrant communities, taught students how to better network and facilitated group discussions for international business people.

Leah's greatest pleasures are making connections and reaching out to build community. Speaking many languages allows her to communicate with more people. She speaks Spanish, Portuguese and some Hebrew and German. She is committed to valuing intergenerational relationships and amplifying kindness.

After becoming a mother, Leah experienced a great shift in her understanding of the world and felt an overwhelming desire to express her need to build community and to help others find and use their voices. In tandem, she joined a kind and passionate poetry community in Portland, Oregon. With the support of the group, poetry has become a way for her to tell stories and to activate others to go out and do something good.

Learn more at www.leahklass.com.

www.ingramcontent.com/pod-product-compliance
Lightning Source LLC
Chambersburg PA
CBHW080942040426
42444CB00015B/3412